States
NEW MEXICO

by Tyler Maine

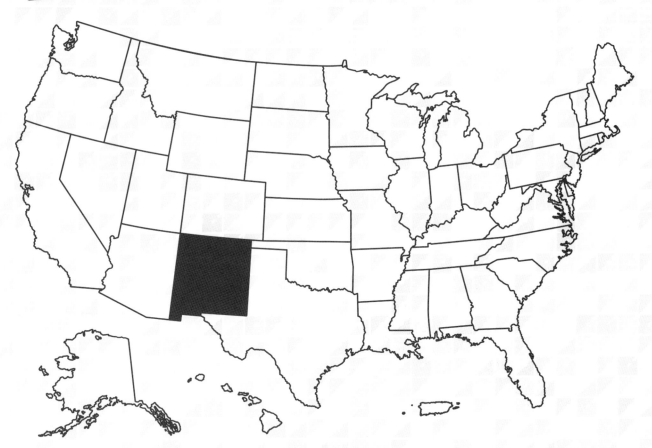

CAPSTONE PRESS
a capstone imprint

Next Page Books are published by Capstone Press,
1710 Roe Crest Drive, North Mankato, Minnesota 56003
www.mycapstone.com

Library of Congress Cataloging-in-Publication Data
Cataloging-in-publication information is on file with the Library of
Congress.
ISBN 978-1-5157-0418-8 (library binding)
ISBN 978-1-5157-0477-5 (paperback)
ISBN 978-1-5157-0529-1 (ebook PDF)

Editorial Credits
Jaclyn Jaycox, editor; Kazuko Collins and Katy LaVigne, designers;
Morgan Walters, media researcher; Tori Abraham, production specialist

Photo Credits
Capstone Press: Angi Gahler, map 4, 7; CriaImages.com: Jay Robert
Nash Collection, middle 19; Dreamstime: Bambi L. Dingman, 9; Getty
Images: AFP/PAUL BUCK, middle 18; iStockphoto: MarinaGold, 27;
Newscom: Album/Oronoz, 25, DanitaDelimont.com Danita Delimont
Photography/Dennis Brack, top 19, Icon SMI/Tony Donaldson, bottom
19, Lou Novick/Cal Sport Media, 29, NANCY STONE/KRT, 14; North
Wind Picture Archives, 12, 26; One Mile Up, Inc., flag, seal 23;
Shutterstock: aceshot1, 16, Dean Fikar, bottom left 8, Doug Meek,
10, Everett Historical, 28, Featureflash, top 18, gary yim, 5, Gimas,
11, Lynne Albright, 6, Matt Jeppson, bottom right 20, (beans) top left
21, middle left 21, Michael E Halstead, 17, Mrs. Loh, bottom right 8,
Natalia Bratslavsky, bottom 24, s_bukley, bottom 18, Shutterstock/
Bildagentur Zoonar GmbH, top right 21, Steve Bower, cover, Tamara
Kulikova, top right 20, (peppers) top left 21, threerocksimages, 7,
Tom Grundy, top left 20, Tom Reichner, middle right 21, Tyler Olson,
15, Warren Price Photography, bottom left 20, Zack Frank, 13,
zhangyang13576997233, top 24; Wikimedia: DaveHood, bottom left 21,
John Phelan, bottom right 21

All design elements by Shutterstock

Printed and bound in China.
0316/CA21600187
012016   009436F16

TABLE OF CONTENTS

Want to take your research further? Ask your librarian if your school subscribes to PebbleGo Next. If so, when you see this helpful symbol ⃝🡒 throughout the book, log onto www.pebblegonext.com for bonus downloads and information.

LOCATION

New Mexico is one of America's southwestern states. It is the country's fifth-largest state in area. To the south are Texas and the country of Mexico. Texas and a small part of Oklahoma lie to the east. To the north is Colorado, and Arizona is to the west. A corner of Utah touches northwest New Mexico. Santa Fe is the state's capital. Other major cities include Albuquerque, Las Cruces, Rio Rancho, Roswell, and Farmington.

PebbleGo Next Bonus!
To print and label your own map, go to www.pebblegonext.com and search keywords:
NM MAP

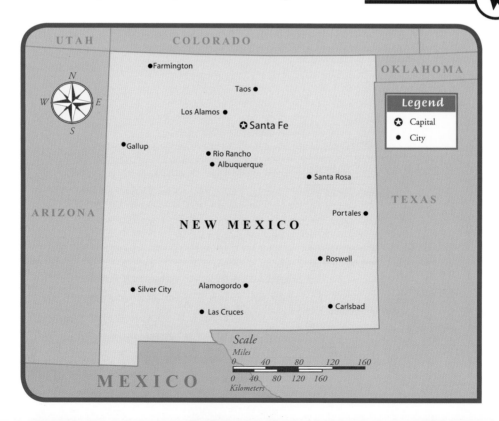

Albuquerque is known as the "Hot Air Balloon Capital of the World."

GEOGRAPHY

New Mexico has some of the world's flattest land and some of the most rugged mountains. The Rocky Mountains and the Colorado Plateau cover northern New Mexico. The Rio Grande, the state's longest river, flows south through the Rocky Mountains. The state's highest point, Wheeler Peak, is slightly east of the Rio Grande. Wheeler Peak rises 13,161 feet (4,011 meters) above sea level. Desert basins lie between mountain ranges in southern New Mexico. The grasslands of the Great Plains cover the eastern third of the state.

PebbleGo Next Bonus! To watch a video about Santa Fe, go to www.pebblegonext.com and search keywords:

NM VIDEO

A view from above the Rio Grande near Santa Fe

6

Wheeler Peak lies in the Sangre de Cristo Mountains in Carson National Forest.

COLORADO PLATEAU

Wheeler Peak

NACIMIENTO MOUNTAINS

JEMEZ MOUNTAINS

Rio Grande

SANGRE DE CRISTO MOUNTAINS

GREAT PLAINS

Canadian River

Pecos River

BASIN AND RANGE REGION

Elephant Butte Lake

SAN ANDRES MOUNTAINS

SACRAMENTO MOUNTAINS

Gila River

WHITE SANDS NATIONAL MONUMENT

CARLSBAD CAVERNS NATIONAL PARK

Red Bluff Reservoir

Legend

▲ Highest Point

◇ Lake

⛰ Mountain Range

▢ National Park or National Monument

〜 River

Scale

Miles

0   40   80   120   160

0   40   80   120   160

Kilometers

WEATHER

People enjoy New Mexico's climate. Summer days are hot. At night the temperature drops. The average temperature in July is about 74 degrees Fahrenheit (23 degrees Celsius). The average temperature in January is 34°F (1°C).

Average High and Low Temperatures (Santa Fe, NM)

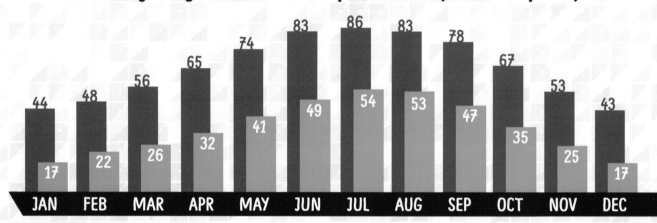

JAN	FEB	MAR	APR	MAY	JUN	JUL	AUG	SEP	OCT	NOV	DEC
44	48	56	65	74	83	86	83	78	67	53	43
17	22	26	32	41	49	54	53	47	35	25	17

LANDMARKS

Santa Fe

This city is the highest state capital in America. It's about 7,000 feet (2,134 m) above sea level. It is also the second-oldest city settled by Europeans in the United States. Only Saint Augustine, Florida, is older.

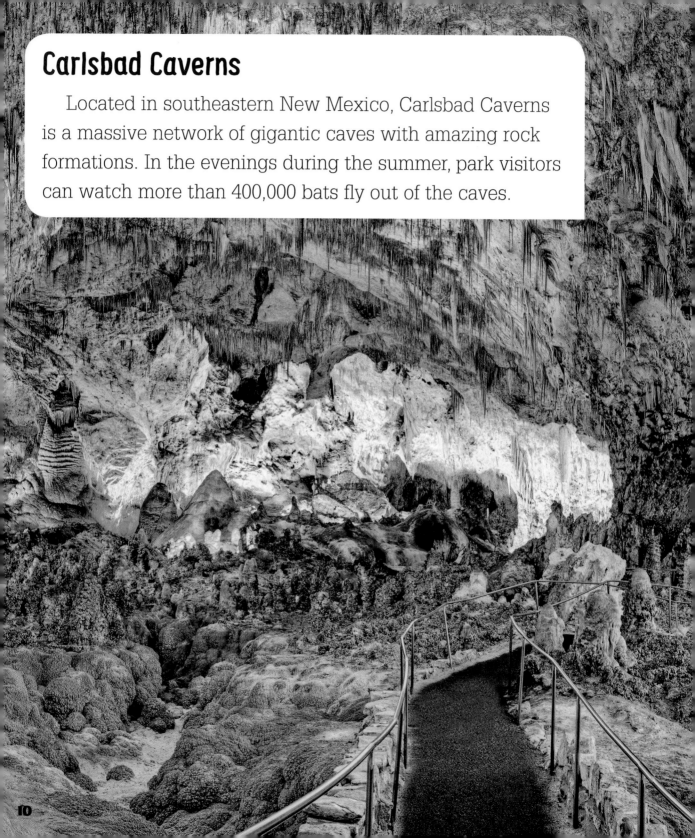

Carlsbad Caverns

Located in southeastern New Mexico, Carlsbad Caverns is a massive network of gigantic caves with amazing rock formations. In the evenings during the summer, park visitors can watch more than 400,000 bats fly out of the caves.

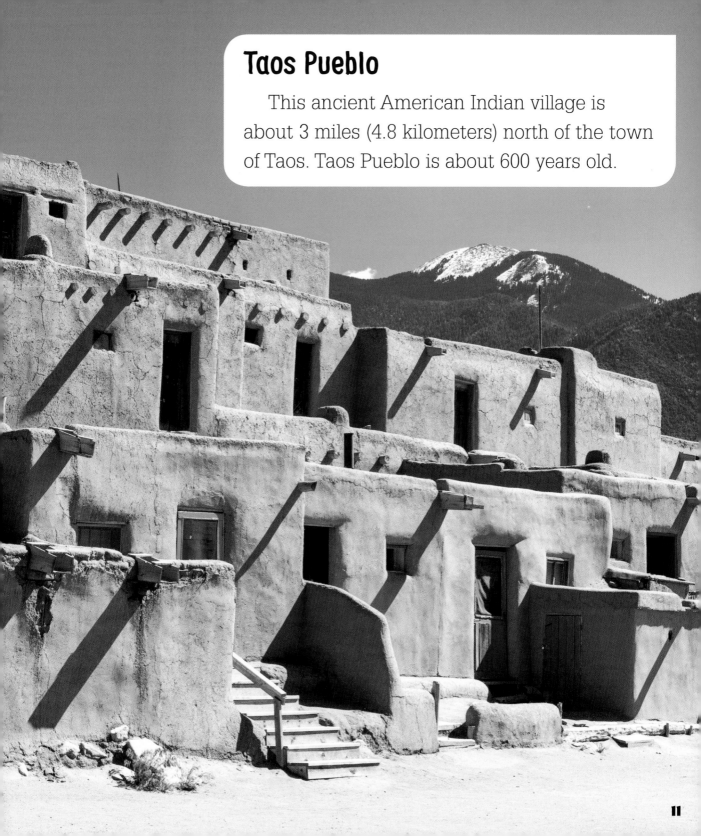

Taos Pueblo

This ancient American Indian village is about 3 miles (4.8 kilometers) north of the town of Taos. Taos Pueblo is about 600 years old.

HISTORY AND GOVERNMENT

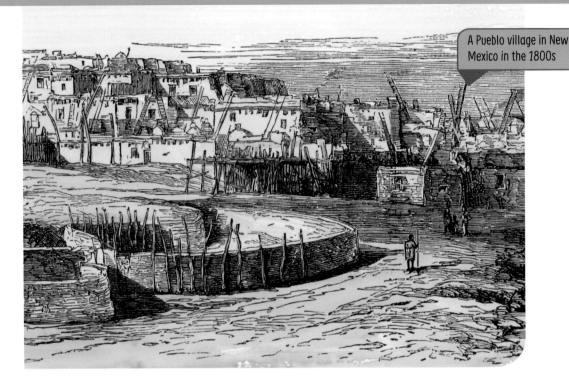

A Pueblo village in New Mexico in the 1800s

From about 500 BC to AD 1200, the Anasazi Indians lived in what is now western New Mexico. By 1300 Pueblo Indians lived along the Rio Grande. The Pueblo, Apache, Comanche, Navajo, and Ute peoples were in the region when Spanish explorers arrived in the 1500s. Juan de Oñate founded the first European colony in New Mexico in 1598.

After Mexico won its freedom from Spain in 1821, New Mexico belonged to Mexico. After the Mexican War (1846–1848), New Mexico became a U.S. property. In 1912 New Mexico became the 47th state.

New Mexico's government has three branches. The governor leads the executive branch. The legislature consists of a 42-member Senate and a 70-member House of Representatives. The court system is the judicial branch. The Pueblo, Navajo, and Jicarilla and Mescalero Apache are self-governing nations in New Mexico.

The state capitol building in Santa Fe is also known as "the Roundhouse." It's the only round capitol building in the United States.

INDUSTRY

Service industries provide the most money for New Mexico's economy. Service industries include government, tourism, health care, and retail stores. Federal government research laboratories and military bases employ many people, playing a major role in the state's economy. Los Alamos National Laboratory is a world leader in nuclear energy research.

Millions of tourists come to New Mexico each year to see the pueblos, historic sites, and American Indian cultural activities.

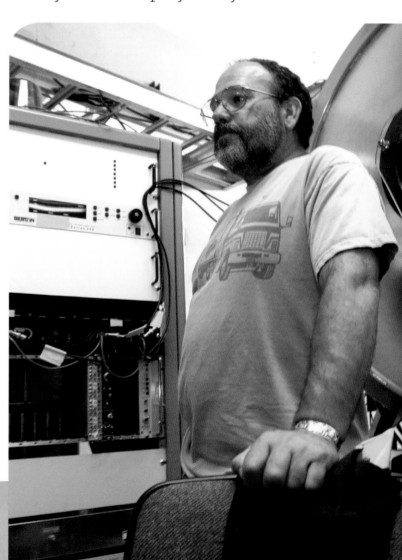

The Los Alamos National Laboratory employs more than 10,000 scientists, engineers, researchers, and more.

New Mexico's leading manufactured products are computer and electronic equipment. Albuquerque is the leading manufacturing center. Other products manufactured in New Mexico include chemicals, clothing, food products, and petroleum products.

The health care industry employs the largest percentage of the workforce in New Mexico.

POPULATION

Today most New Mexico residents are descendants of the three main groups of people who settled the state. The Apache, Navajo, and Pueblo peoples make up the state's American Indian population. Most of the area's early settlers were descendants of Spanish colonists, along with Mexicans who moved north from Mexico. Today there are almost 1 million Hispanics living in New Mexico. Anglo-Americans are the third group of the state's three main cultures. Anglo-Americans are white people who do not have a Spanish background. A small number of New Mexico's residents are Asian or African-American.

Population by Ethnicity

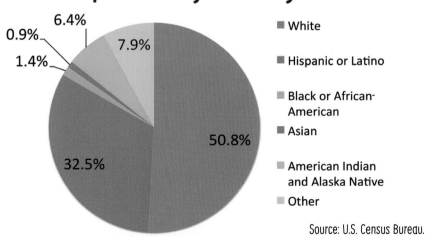

- White — 50.8%
- Hispanic or Latino — 32.5%
- Black or African-American
- Asian
- American Indian and Alaska Native
- Other

6.4%
0.9%
7.9%
1.4%

Source: U.S. Census Bureau.

Albuquerque hosts the largest balloon festival in the world.

FAMOUS PEOPLE

William Hanna (1910–2001) was a cartoonist who worked with Joseph Barbera. They created the animated characters Yogi Bear, Scooby-Doo, and Tom and Jerry. He was born in Melrose.

Nancy Lopez (1957–) is a professional golfer. She was the first Hispanic player to win a Ladies Professional Golf Association (LPGA) tournament in 1978. She was born in California and grew up in Roswell, where an elementary school has been named for her.

Demi Moore (1962–) is an actress. Her movies include *Ghost* (1990), *G.I. Jane* (1997), and *Charlie's Angels: Full Throttle* (2003). She was born as Demi Guynes in Roswell.

Georgia O'Keeffe (1887–1986) was an artist who painted huge pictures of flowers, desert scenes, and animal bones. She was born in Wisconsin and later moved to New Mexico.

Popé (1630–1692) led the Pueblo Revolt of 1680. After the Spaniards were driven out, he worked to restore Pueblo culture.

Al Unser Sr. (1939–) is a retired IndyCar series driver. He won the Indianapolis 500 four times. His brother, Bobby Unser (1934–) has won the Indy 500 three times. Al's son, Al Unser Jr. (1962–) has won the Indy 500 twice. The Albuquerque racecar drivers have also won many other races.

STATE SYMBOLS

Tree

piñon

Flower

yucca

Bird

chaparral (roadrunner)

Fish

cutthroat trout

PebbleGo Next Bonus! To make New Mexico's state cookie, go to www.pebblegonext.com and search keywords:

NM RECIPE

Vegetables

chile and *frijoles* (beans)

Grass

blue grama

Reptile

whiptail lizard

Animal

black bear

Insect

tarantula hawk wasp

Cookie

biscochito

21

FAST FACTS

STATEHOOD
1912

CAPITAL ☆
Santa Fe

LARGEST CITY •
Albuquerque

SIZE
121,298 square miles (314,160 square kilometers) land area (2010 U.S. Census Bureau)

POPULATION
2,085,287 (2013 U.S. Census estimate)

STATE NICKNAME
Land of Enchantment

STATE MOTTO
"Crescit Eundo," meaning "It grows as it goes"

STATE SEAL

New Mexico adopted its state seal in 1913, one year after becoming a state. Two eagles are on the seal. The American bald eagle stands for the United States. The eagle holds three arrows in its claws. The eagle's wing shields a smaller Mexican brown eagle. This image represents New Mexico Territory joining the United States. The brown eagle holds a cactus and snake. They stand for an ancient Aztec myth. A scroll below the eagles shows the state's motto, "Crescit Eundo." This Latin phrase means "It grows as it goes."

PebbleGo Next Bonus!
To print and color your own flag, go to www.pebblegonext.com and search keywords:
NM FLAG

STATE FLAG

New Mexico adopted its flag in 1925. A red Zia symbol is in the center of the flag. The Zia is an ancient sun symbol of the Zia Indians. Four lines extend from each side of the circle. One group of lines stands for north, south, east, and west. Another group stands for the seasons of the year. Four lines represent the four parts of the day. The last four lines represent childhood, youth, middle years, and old age.

MINING PRODUCTS

natural gas, petroleum, coal, potash, copper, limestone, molybdenum, portland cement, sand and gravel

MANUFACTURED GOODS

computer and electronic equipment, food products, chemicals, fabricated metal products, nonmetallic mineral products, petroleum and coal products, paper, transportation equipment

FARM PRODUCTS

beef cattle, sheep, milk, hay, chile peppers, pecans

PebbleGo Next Bonus!
To learn the lyrics to the state song, go to www.pebblegonext.com and search keywords:

NM SONG

NEW MEXICO TIMELINE

1500
The Navajo and Apache people come to New Mexico from the north.

1536
Spanish explorer Álvar Núñez Cabeza de Vaca enters New Mexico from Texas.

1540
Francisco Vásquez de Coronado explores New Mexico for Spain.

1598
Juan de Oñate establishes San Juan, New Mexico's first permanent Spanish colony.

1620 The Pilgrims establish a colony in the New World in present-day Massachusetts.

1680 Pueblo Indians in northern New Mexico revolt against the oppressive rule of the Spanish.

1821 Mexico wins independence from Spain; New Mexico becomes a colony of Mexico.

1848 The Mexican War ends, and New Mexico becomes part of the United States.

1850 U.S. Congress creates the New Mexico Territory.

1861–1865

The Union and the Confederacy fight the Civil War, including battles in New Mexico, where the Confederacy occupies the southern part of the state and the Union rules in the north.

1886

The Apache Wars, during which Apaches resist the U.S. military's attempts to move them to reservations, end with the surrender of Apache leader Geronimo.

1912

On January 6 New Mexico becomes the 47th state.

1914–1918

World War I is fought; the United States enters the war in 1917.

1922 Oil is discovered in New Mexico.

1939–1945 World War II is fought; the United States enters the war in 1941.

1945 The world's first atomic bomb, which would later be used to end World War II when the Allies dropped two atomic bombs on Japan, is detonated in a test explosion in the White Sands Desert near Alamogordo.

1982 The U.S. Supreme Court rules that American Indian nations may charge taxes on minerals mined from their lands, giving them more control over the mineral rights on government land allotted to American Indians.

1994 The North American Free Trade Agreement increases trade between New Mexico and Mexico.

2011 Susana Martinez becomes New Mexico's first female governor and the first Hispanic woman to serve as a U.S. governor.

2012 Forest fires burn 300,000 acres (121,000 hectares) in the Gila National Forest in western New Mexico.

2015 The New Mexico Museum of Natural History and Science unveils the first baby Pentaceratops skull ever discovered.

Glossary

culture *(KUHL-chuhr)*—a people's way of life, ideas, art, customs, and traditions

descend *(dee-SEND)*—if you are descended from someone, you belong to a later generation of the same family

executive *(ig-ZE-kyuh-tiv)*—the branch of government that makes sure laws are followed

industry *(IN-duh-stree)*—a business which produces a product or provides a service

judicial *(joo-DISH-uhl)*—to do with the branch of government that explains and interprets the laws

legislature *(LEJ-iss-lay-chur)*—a group of elected officials who have the power to make or change laws for a country or state

massive *(MASS-iv)*—large, heavy, and solid

mineral *(MIN-ur-uhl)*—a substance found in nature that is not made by a plant or animal

petroleum *(puh-TROH-lee-uhm)*—an oily liquid found below the earth's surface used to make gasoline, heating oil, and many other products

tourism *(TOOR-i-zuhm)*—the business of taking care of visitors to a country or place

Read More

Bjorklund, Ruth. *New Mexico: The Land of Enchantment.* It's My State! New York: Cavendish Square, 2016.

Fretland VanVoorst, Jenny. *What's Great About New Mexico?* Our Great States. Minneapolis: Lerner Publications, 2014.

Ganeri, Anita. *United States of America: A Benjamin Blog and His Inquisitive Dog Investigation.* Country Guides. Chicago: Heinemann Raintree, 2015.

Internet Sites

FactHound offers a safe, fun way to find Internet sites related to this book. All of the sites on FactHound have been researched by our staff.

Here's all you do:

Visit *www.facthound.com*

Type in this code: 9781515704188

 Check out projects, games and lots more at
www.capstonekids.com

Critical Thinking Using the Common Core

1. What is New Mexico's weather like? (Key Ideas and Details)

2. What do millions of tourists come to New Mexico each year to see? (Key Ideas and Details)

3. According to the pie chart on page 16, what percentage of New Mexico's population is Hispanic or Latino? (Craft and Structure)

Index